Farmyard Friends

Pigs

Camilla de la Bédoyère

QEB Publishing

Editor: Eve Marleau
Designer: Melissa Alaverdy
Picture Researcher:
    Maria Joannou

Copyright © QEB Publishing, Inc. 2009

Published in the United States by
QEB Publishing, Inc.
3 Wrigley, Suite A
Irvine, CA 92618

www.qed-publishing.co.uk

Library of Congress Cataloging-in-Publication Data

De la Bédoyère, Camilla.   DEC 2 0 2010
  Pigs / Camilla de la Bédoyère.
     p. cm. -- (QEB farmyard friends)
  Includes index.
  ISBN 978-1-59566-939-1 (library binding)
  1. Swine--Juvenile literature. I. Title.
  SF395.5.D44 2011
  636.4--dc22

                                    2010001142

Printed in China

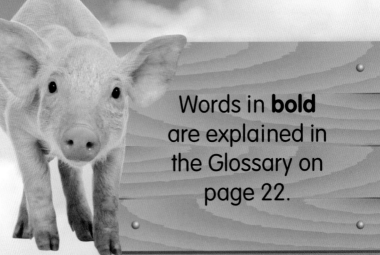

Words in **bold**
are explained in
the Glossary on
page 22.

Picture credits
(t=top, b=bottom, l=left, r=right, c=center,
fc=front cover)

Alamy Images Ulrich Baumgarten/Vario images 10l,
Wayne Hutchinson 21t; Corbis Robert Polett/AgStock
Images 8-9; **Getty Images** Workbook Stock/John
Zoiner 6-7, Dorling Kindersley/Simon Clay 11t,
Dorling Kindersley 12t; **Photolibrary** Philippe Body
4l, Juniors Bildarchiv 4-5, 5t, 13t, 14t, 18-19, 20-21,
Index Stock Imagery/Grant Heilman Photography Inc
9t, Tips Italia/Bildagentur RM 10-11, Age Fotostock/
EA. Janes 12-13, 14b, Imagebroker.net/Michael Krabs
15c, Imagebroker.net/Helmut Meyer zur Capellen
16-17, Superstock/Clyde M Slade 17t; **Rex Features**
East News 7t, Jussi Nukari 15t; **Shutterstock** Ulrich
Mueller cr, JinYoung Lee cl, Eric Isselée 2t, Antonio
Jorge Nunes 2-3, MisterElements 3t, 5b, 7b, 11b,
12b, 15b, 17b, 19b, 20b, Dario Sabljak 8l, Jonson 19t,
Graeme Dawes 20t, Joy Brown 22b, Aleks.K 22-23,
Luis Louro 24b.

Contents

What are pigs?

Pigs are mammals. All mammals have hairy bodies and feed their babies with milk.

Pigs have small eyes but their noses are large. They have a very good sense of smell.

tail

Pigs have barrel-shaped bodies, thin legs, and big heads. ⇨

trotter

⇧ A pig's trotter is cloven. This means it has two parts.

Pigs have hoofed feet and walk on two toes, like sheep and cows. Their feet are called trotters.

tusk

head

shoulder

snout

↑ Wild pigs have more hair than farm pigs. They are smaller, faster, and often have **tusks**.

Farmyard Fact!

A male pig is called a boar. Female pigs are called sows. Baby pigs are called piglets.

Pigs on the Farm

Pigs are also known as hogs or swine. They are kept on farms for their meat.

They live in family groups, called herds. In the wild, they live in woods where they **forage**, or look, for food.

⇩ Farm pigs like to spend time outdoors.

Pigs can weigh up to 1,000 pounds (450 kilograms) and are about 28 inches (70 centimeters) tall – that's nearly as big as a child!

Pigs are very clean animals. Sows are friendly, too.

Farmyard fact!

Pigs do not like hot weather because they cannot sweat. Sweating helps an animal cool down.

Where do pigs live?

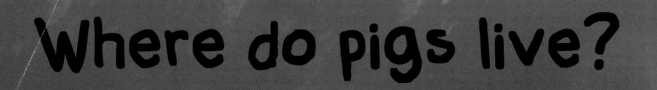

Most pigs live in large pigpens or in fields on farms. There can be several pens in one barn.

Sows are often kept in pens together. Sometimes, sows are kept alone in small pens called stalls.

Boars are kept in separate pens, because they often fight with each other. Their pens have high fences so they cannot jump over them.

← These sows are resting in their pens.

Some farmers give their ➡ pigs straw to sleep on.

⬇ Large indoor pig farms are called **piggeries**. Pig food is stored in big metal tanks.

Farmyard Fact!

Pigs used to live on small farms, but now many of them live in piggeries. Thousands of pigs live in just one piggery.

What do pigs eat?

Pigs can eat many things, such as meat, fruit, and grass. Animals that eat different foods are called omnivores.

Pigs get their water from **drinkers.** A sow can drink more than 8 gallons (30 liters) of water every day.

⇐ This young pig is sucking water from a drinker.

Pigs eat food from troughs.
Most pigs eat pellets that contain
vitamins to keep them healthy.

⇓ Pellets are made from
cereals and vitamins.

⇓ Pigs like to walk in fields
where they can find fresh
grass to eat.

Farmyard Fact!

A pig has 44 teeth. Wild pigs
grow large teeth, called
tusks. Boars use their tusks
to fight each other.

Living outside

Some pigs live in outdoor shelters in fields. Their shelters are called sties, huts, or arcs.

The shelters protect the pigs from hot, cold, and wet weather. The pigs eat food, such as grass and roots, in the field.

← This type of metal shelter is called an arc.

Farmyard fact!

Truffles are a type of rare mushroom that grows underground. Some farmers train pigs to find the truffles using their sense of smell.

Pigs like to lie in mud. It keeps their skin cool, and stops them from getting sunburned.

⇧ **Free-range** piglets can stay with their mother.

⇩ These pigs are called outdoor-reared, or free-range, because they live outside.

The life cycle of a pig

Sows are pregnant for about four months before they give birth. Baby pigs are called piglets.

Sows can give birth to a litter of about 10 piglets at a time. The piglets become adults at about two years old.

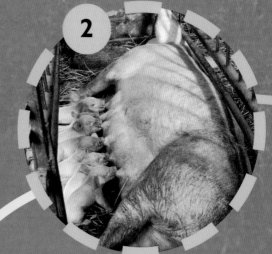

⇧ When piglets are born, they drink their mother's milk. It helps them to grow and stay healthy.

⇦ The farmer puts the sow into a **farrowing** stall about one week before she is due to give birth.

3 ⇐ The piglets live in a nursery pen for five to 10 weeks.

⇩ When they are about 10 weeks old, the piglets can go to the sheds or fields. Then the life cycle begins again.

4

Farmyard Fact!

Piglets move into a separate area when their mother wants to sleep. Otherwise, she might crush them!

Life on the farm

Pigs spend most of the day eating, drinking, and resting.

Farmers clean the pens regularly, removing all the dirty straw and putting new straw down. The pigs like to sniff around in the straw.

Inspectors check that the pigs are kept in clean, safe pens, and that they are healthy. When they are old enough, the pigs are taken from the farm, and sold for meat.

Farm pigs can eat or drink ⇨ whenever they want to.

⇦ Young pigs like to be together. Most pens hold pigs that are all the same age.

Farmyard fact!

Pigs are so smart they can learn how to open farm gates. Some people like pigs so much they keep them as pets!

Why do we farm pigs?

Most pigs are kept on farms for their meat. The meat that comes from pigs is called pork.

Pork is packaged and sold to supermarkets or stores. Pork can also be used to make foods such as sausages and bacon.

⬇ Pigs live on the farm until it is time for them to be sold for meat.

Some pork is used to make ham and bacon. The meat is stored in dry salt or salty water, before other flavors are added to it. This type of pork is called **cured meat**.

⇑ Ham is a type of cured meat.

Farmyard Fact!

People have been eating sausages for thousands of years. Most sausages are made from pork and cereals.

Breeds of pig

There are many different types of pig. Each type is called a breed.

Large white pigs are one of the world's most popular breeds. Farmers are able to keep them outdoors, or in pig sheds.

⇐ Large white sows are very good mothers.

large white pig

Farmyard fact!

Mangalitza pigs are covered in a layer of curly fur. It helps them to stay warm during long, cold winters.

Kune kune pigs are rare. Their hair can be straight or curly, and it is often spotted. They have short legs and small snouts.

The name of a Kune kune pig ⇨ means "fat and round."

Mangalitza pigs are kept on farms in Europe. Their meat is used for ham, sausage, and bacon.

Mangalitza pigs are also known ⬇ as woolly pigs.

Mangalitza pig

21

Glossary

Cereal
This is a type of food that comes from grains, such as wheat, oats, and corn.

Cured meat
This meat has been changed by adding salt to it.

Drinker
Pigs can get fresh water from drinkers.

Farrowing
This is the time when a sow gives birth to her piglets.

Forage
When animals forage, they are searching for food.

Free-range
Animals that are able to live outdoors, and have plenty of space, are called free-range.

Inspector
This person checks that farm animals are being kept in good, clean, and healthy places.

Piggery
This is a large indoor pig farm.

Tusk
This is a long, pointed tooth.

Vitamin
Living things need vitamins to grow and to stay healthy. Food contains vitamins.

Index

Notes for parents and teachers

Look through the book together, talk about the pictures, and find new words in the Glossary.

It is fun to find ways that animals are similar, or different from one another—and observing these things is a core science skill. Children could draw pictures of animals with four legs, or ones that eat plants, for example, and go on to identify those that are both plant-eaters and four-legged.

Talk about the basic needs that animals and humans share, such as food, space, and shelter. Encourage the child to think about how wild animals get their food and find shelter.

Be prepared for questions about how animals become the meat that we eat. It helps children understand this part of the food chain if they can see it in context: all animals live and die, and farm animals are bred for this purpose.